IT

STARTS

WITH

ME

COURAGEOUS QUESTIONS
FOR THE FEARLESS LEADER'S HEART

IT STARTS WITH ME

COURAGEOUS QUESTIONS FOR THE LEADER'S HEART

An Empowerment Embassy Collection
for Self-Reflection

Compiled by Laura R. Brown

Printed in the United States of America
First Printing, 2017
ISBN 978-1-941749-74-6
Library of Congress Control Number 2017913783
4-P Publishing
Chattanooga, TN 374

About
The Empowerment Embassy

Dr. David L. Banks, Pastor

- Our mission is "Equipping Leaders with Kingdom Principles to Impact the 8 Fields."
- Our mandate is to go out into the world to preach the gospel of the Kingdom of Heaven and teach others to live by Kingdom Principles.
- We are purpose-driven, and we have a desire for the Church to return to its original design.

At the Empowerment Embassy, we show you how to use Kingdom Principles to Create Influence in your life and to Transform Earth to reflect Heaven.

The Principles We Believe:

Principles, Order & Original Design - When God created Heaven and Earth, He set certain laws and principles to govern the Earth realm. When we begin to live by the Principles of God instead of man-made religion, we work with God to create order and return Earth to its original design.

The Kingdom of Heaven, The Head, and the Host Country -The Kingdom of Heaven is where God reigns, and He has given Earth to mankind (Psalm 155:16). The Head Country is Heaven, and the Host Country is Earth. We have a mandate to transform Earth back into what God intended it to be.

Salvation & Righteousness - Salvation is not a one-time emotional experience. It is a transfer into and access to operate within the Kingdom Realm. Righteousness is living the way God designed us to live, instead of the way the world has conditioned us to live.

Purpose - Your purpose is God's original intent for creating you.

The Church & The Embassy - The church is the Body of Christ. The Embassy is the building where Kingdom partners meet to worship and receive education and information from Heaven (the Head Country)

Partners & Ambassadors - An ambassador is one who represents the King. As an ambassador, we are representatives of the Kingdom of Heaven. At the Empowerment Embassy, we are partners instead of members. As members, we only join an organization. When we become partners, we take a deeper level of commitment and ownership. As a partner of the Empowerment Embassy, we are leaders and take ownership of God's purpose, and it becomes our responsibility to spread His message.

The 8 Fields - Impacting the 8 Fields is our strategy for influencing the world and re-establishing order on Earth. The 8 fields are Home, Education, Business, Government, Medical, Ministry, Arts, and Regions. When each partner learns how to influence their individual fields, we ensure the Kingdom message spreads throughout the world.

Ministry | Church
Home | Family, Marriage, Children
Medical | Health, Emotional, Physical
Arts | Entertainment, Technology, Media
Government | Social, City, State, Federal
Business | Entrepreneurship and Commerce
Regions | Communities, Neighborhood, States, Countries, Continents
Education | Teaching and Applying the Principles in Schools & Universities

A NOTE FROM THE PUBLISHER

IT STARTS WITH ME is an Empowerment Embassy collaboration birthed from a message during one of our weekly training sessions. As we highlighted the need for leaders to have personal accountability in our lives when things go in the wrong direction, we shared personal self-reflection questions to identify the root causes of our experiences and life choices. I have given credit to each person who submitted a question.

The quotes following the questions are for added consideration as you answer the questions. Use of quotes is not an endorsement of the view, ideologies or beliefs of the person quoted. Some names you may recognize. I encourage you to research the identities of the names that are not familiar to you.

I hope you find these questions insightful, thought-provoking, encouraging, and life changing. Remember, no matter what you do in life, you are a leader because someone is following you whether you realize it or not. Make it a priority to be the version of a leader you can!

Laura R. Brown
4-P Publishing

INTRODUCTION

- Do you find yourself unable to move forward in life?

- Do you need help overcoming repeated setbacks?

- Are you ready to face some core truths about yourself?

- Do you want to cultivate the leader's heart in you?

Be courageous and take a dive into self-discovery questions to challenge and motivate you to go deeper and get to the heart of what may be holding you back from personal and professional success and freedom. Amplify your leadership quotient and expand your influence through self-examination. Examining your behavior, thoughts and feelings will help you identify patterns in your life and give you insights into areas in need of spiritual, mental, emotional, or physical transformation.

IT STARTS WITH ME contains self-reflection questions addressing various core areas of your life: identity, purpose, personal growth, lifestyle, beliefs, relationships, health, wealth, and worldview. There are also journal pages to answer the questions. Most questions are in no particular sequence, so you have the freedom to begin on any page you like. The last question in the chapter is a culmination of your self-reflection experiences and how you have changed. Each journal page ends with a call to action statement. This is your opportunity to challenge yourself to think or act differently as a result of your self-reflection journey. There are blank journal pages in the back of the book for you to create your own self-reflection questions.

While you are free to answer the questions in any way you like, here is a suggestion to get the most of your experience. When answering the questions, prepare to do three things:

- Look Back - recognize past behavior/thought patterns
- Look Inward - identify root causes of those patterns
- Look Forward - develop a plan to create new behavior/thought patterns

To enhance your visual experience, you will see various fonts used for each question. Have fun with them by coloring them and make this a unique journal that reflects you!

Ways to use this book:

- Personal Journal
- Meditation
- Conversation Starters
- Group Discussions
- Leadership Training
- Life Coaching Sessions

Grab some pens, colored pencils or markers and embark upon your unique journey into your deepest thoughts and uncover the hidden things of your heart.

Remember, as a leader, IT STARTS WITH YOU!

To connect with The Empowerment Embassy of Chattanooga, TN go to www.theempowermentembassy.com or you may e-mail us at theempowermentchurch@gmail.com

You can purchase additional copies of this book at Amazon.com. Look for the Kindle version for on-the-go versatility.

To purchase twenty or more copies for a bulk discount, contact the publisher at coachlaurabrown@swatbookcamp.com

IT STARTS WITH ME

WHAT ARE THE TOP FIVE CONCERNS I HAVE IN MY LIFE RIGHT NOW? WHY DO THEY CONCERN ME?

- Dr. Sharon Cannon

"When we are no longer able to change a situation, we are challenged to change ourselves." – Viktor Frankl

Date: _____

_____

_____

_____

_____

_____

_____

_____

_____

_____

_____

_____

_____

_____

_____

_____

_____

_____

_____

_____

_____

_____

_____

_____

_____

MY ACTION STATEMENT:

Place dots on the chart that correspond to your level of fulfillment and consistency in each core area of your life. Connect the dots. What areas need improvement?

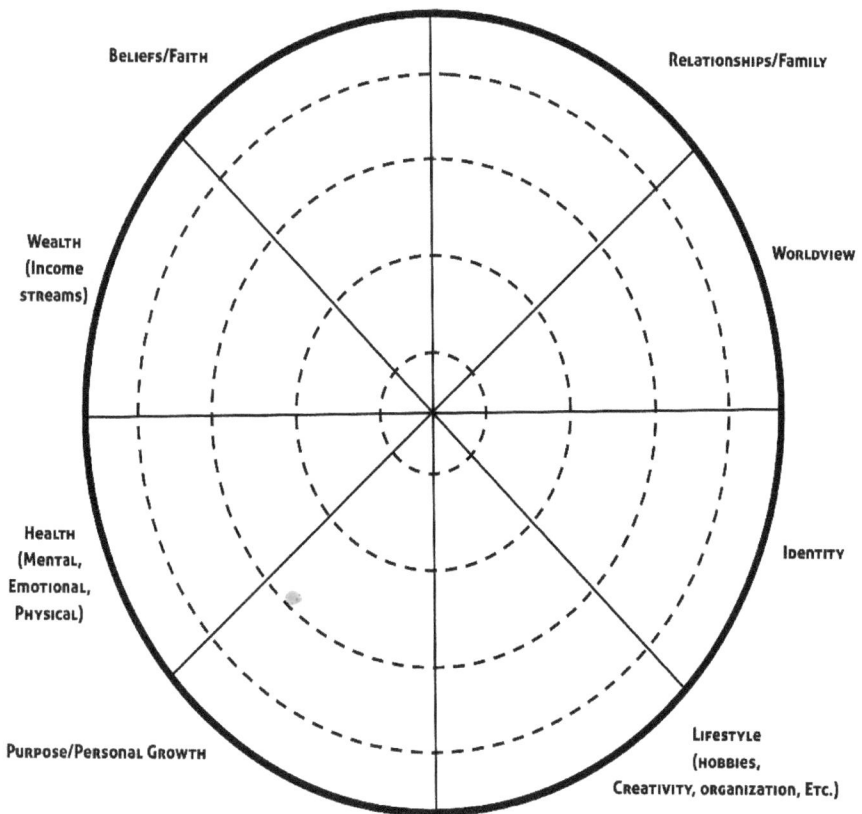

Beliefs/Faith

Relationships/Family

Wealth (Income streams)

Worldview

Health (Mental, Emotional, Physical)

Identity

Purpose/Personal Growth

Lifestyle (hobbies, Creativity, organization, Etc.)

"Most times we are so focused on what we need to change on the outside that we forget the inside needs the most work."

– Pauline Seaport

Date: _____

_____

_____

_____

_____

_____

_____

_____

_____

_____

_____

_____

_____

_____

_____

_____

_____

_____

_____

_____

_____

_____

_____

_____

_____

_____

_____

MY ACTION STATEMENT:

DO I KNOW WHAT I AM DESIGNED TO DO?

-Tarrell Whiteside

"A wind that blows aimlessly is no good to anyone."
— Rick Riordan

(See Purpose Discovery worksheet at the end of the journal pages to discover your purpose and create your personal mission statement)

Date: _____

_____

_____

_____

_____

_____

_____

_____

_____

_____

_____

_____

_____

_____

_____

_____

_____

_____

_____

_____

_____

_____

_____

_____

_____

_____

_____

MY ACTION STATEMENT:

Five Questions to Discover Your Purpose

1. What do you see in society that burdens you or grieves you?

2. What group of people are you passionate about? **(Circle one)**

People in general	Children	Couples	Professionals
Non-Christians	Teens	Families	Seniors
An ethnic group	Women	Singles	Adults
Single family households	Men	Religious groups	Other_____

3. What would be your message to this group? What is your objective (create a one sentence statement)?

4. Choose words of how you would like to help the above group (circle two).

Motivate	Create	Discover	Teach
Encourage	Comfort	Lead	Guide
Empower	Influence	Impact	Develop
Nurture	Impart	Repair	Support
Challenge	Equip	Change	Coach
Serve	Develop	Organize	Counsel

Other_____

5. What do you want this group to become because of your influence?

Examples:

To live a successful life

To be productive

Maximize their potential

To obtain more out of their lives

To reach higher goals

Other_____

The Purpose Code

Take the answers to the questions and follow the Code:
4,2,3,5

4.

2.

3.

5.

Example: To motivate and empower people to discover their purpose and potential so they can live fulfilling lives.

My purpose is: *(use next page to test different versions of your statement. Write the one that resonates with you the most, below).*

Purpose Discovery Statement Test Page.

(use this page to test various wordings of your statement. Once you are satisfied, enter it on the previous page.)

Am I living TRUE to my purpose?

-Laura Brown

"A lot of the conflict you have in your life exists simply because you're not living in alignment; you're not being true to yourself." – Steve Maraboli

Date: _____

_____

_____

_____

_____

_____

_____

_____

_____

_____

_____

_____

_____

_____

_____

_____

_____

_____

_____

_____

_____

_____

_____

_____

_____

_____

_____

MY ACTION STATEMENT:

Am I willing to be my AUTHENTIC self, even if others cannot accept me?

— Erika Hughes

"Be yourself--not your idea of what you think somebody else's idea of yourself should be." -Henry David Thoreau

Date: _____

_____

_____

_____

_____

_____

_____

_____

_____

_____

_____

_____

_____

_____

_____

_____

_____

_____

_____

_____

_____

_____

_____

_____

_____

_____

_____

_____

MY ACTION STATEMENT:

Have I ever minimized my talents to appease others? How did it make me feel?

-Laura Brown

"Don't you dare shrink yourself for someone else's comfort,
Do not become small for people who refuse to grow." – Anonymous

Date: _____

_____
_____
_____
_____
_____
_____
_____
_____
_____
_____
_____
_____
_____
_____
_____
_____
_____
_____
_____
_____
_____
_____
_____
_____
_____
_____
_____
_____

MY ACTION STATEMENT:

How COMFORTABLE am I RECEIVING from others

(gifts, help, compliments, assistance...)?

"Gracious acceptance is an art – an art which most never bother to cultivate. We think that we have to learn how to give, but we forget about accepting things, which can be much harder than giving... Accepting another person's gift is allowing him to express his feelings for you."

– Alexander McCall Smith

Date: _____

_____
_____
_____
_____
_____
_____
_____
_____
_____
_____
_____
_____
_____
_____
_____
_____
_____
_____
_____
_____
_____
_____
_____
_____
_____
_____
_____
_____

MY ACTION STATEMENT:

Am I taking care of MYSELF? (physically, emotionally, mentally)?

-Multiple Contributors

"How we care for ourselves gives our brain messages that shape our self-worth so we must care for ourselves in every way, every day." - Sam Owen

Date: _____

_____
_____
_____
_____
_____
_____
_____
_____
_____
_____
_____
_____
_____
_____
_____
_____
_____
_____
_____
_____
_____
_____
_____
_____
_____
_____
_____

MY ACTION STATEMENT:

How do I

RECHARGE

my mental, physical,

& emotional

batteries?

- Dr. David Banks, April Boozer, Laura Brown, & Trina McKinney

"Relax, Recharge and Reflect. Sometimes it's OK to do nothing."
- Izey Victoria Odias

Date: _____

_____

_____

_____

_____

_____

_____

_____

_____

_____

_____

_____

_____

_____

_____

_____

_____

_____

_____

_____

_____

_____

_____

_____

_____

_____

_____

_____

_____

MY ACTION STATEMENT:

How can I ensure REST is one of my priorities?

-Laura Brown

"There is virtue in work, and there is virtue in rest.
Use both and overlook neither." -Alan Cohen

Date: _____

_____

_____

_____

_____

_____

_____

_____

_____

_____

_____

_____

_____

_____

_____

_____

_____

_____

_____

_____

_____

_____

_____

_____

_____

_____

_____

_____

_____

MY ACTION STATEMENT:

Am I living by my internal standards or by external situations?

~ Sylvia Banks

"It's not hard to make decisions when you know what your values are."
– Roy Disney

Date: _____

_____
_____
_____
_____
_____
_____
_____
_____
_____
_____
_____
_____
_____
_____
_____
_____
_____
_____
_____
_____
_____
_____
_____
_____
_____
_____
_____

MY ACTION STATEMENT:

Am I letting issues that are OUT OF MY CONTROL cause stress in my life?

-Laura Brown

"Incredible change happens in your life when you decide to take control of what you do have power over instead of craving control over what you don't." – Steve Maraboli

Date: _____

_____

_____

_____

_____

_____

_____

_____

_____

_____

_____

_____

_____

_____

_____

_____

_____

_____

_____

_____

_____

_____

_____

_____

_____

_____

_____

MY ACTION STATEMENT:

HOW CAN I CONTROL MY reaction TO A NEGATIVE SITUATION?

– Kathy White

"If a man realizes who he is, he will not react to the negative things surrounding him" - Sunday Adelaja

40

Date: _____

_____

_____

_____

_____

_____

_____

_____

_____

_____

_____

_____

_____

_____

_____

_____

_____

_____

_____

_____

_____

_____

_____

_____

_____

_____

_____

_____

_____

MY ACTION STATEMENT:

What decisions have I been avoiding?

-Laura Brown & Tarrell Whiteside

"Not making a decision means forgoing an opportunity."

- Auliq Ice

Date: _____

_____

_____

_____

_____

_____

_____

_____

_____

_____

_____

_____

_____

_____

_____

_____

_____

_____

_____

_____

_____

_____

_____

_____

_____

_____

_____

MY ACTION STATEMENT:

IF NOT NOW, WHEN?

-Patricia Robinson

"He who refuses to embrace a unique opportunity loses the prize as surely as if he had failed." – William James

"If a window of opportunity appears, don't pull down the shade."
-Thomas J. Peters

Date: _____

_____
_____
_____
_____
_____
_____
_____
_____
_____
_____
_____
_____
_____
_____
_____
_____
_____
_____
_____
_____
_____
_____
_____
_____
_____
_____
_____

MY ACTION STATEMENT:

WHAT ACTIVITY, PERSON, OR ASSOCIATIONS HAVE BEEN LIFE-GIVING?

-Laura Brown

"Spend time with people who know how to use their days well. Just as iron sharpens iron, positive people will inspire you to be positive." – Rhianna

Date: _____

_____
_____
_____
_____
_____
_____
_____
_____
_____
_____
_____
_____
_____
_____
_____
_____
_____
_____
_____
_____
_____
_____
_____
_____
_____

MY ACTION STATEMENT:

What activity, person, or associations have been life-draining or toxic?

-LAURA BROWN

"Life is too short to waste your time with people who waste their own time." -Anonymous

Date: _____

_____

_____

_____

_____

_____

_____

_____

_____

_____

_____

_____

_____

_____

_____

_____

_____

_____

_____

_____

_____

_____

_____

_____

_____

_____

_____

_____

_____

MY ACTION STATEMENT:

When am I most likely to feel alone? How do I cope with feeling alone?

- Dammon Dunn

"Loneliness expresses the pain of being alone, and solitude expresses the glory of being alone." –Paul Tillich

"God makes a home for the lonely; He leads out the prisoners into prosperity, Only the rebellious dwell in a parched land." –Psalm 68:6 NASB

Date: _____

_____

_____

_____

_____

_____

_____

_____

_____

_____

_____

_____

_____

_____

_____

_____

_____

_____

_____

_____

_____

_____

_____

_____

_____

_____

_____

_____

_____

MY ACTION STATEMENT:

When I say "NO"!

Do I feel GUILTY or POWERFUL? Why?

-Laura Brown

"The difference between successful people and really successful people is that really successful people say 'No' to almost everything." - Warren Buffett

Date: _____

_____
_____
_____
_____
_____
_____
_____
_____
_____
_____
_____
_____
_____
_____
_____
_____
_____
_____
_____
_____
_____
_____
_____
_____
_____
_____
_____
_____

MY ACTION STATEMENT:

What kind of role model am I to my children? and others?

~ Sylvia Banks

"Children have never been very good at listening to their elders, but they have never failed to imitate them." — James Baldwin

"I don't want to be a supermodel; I want to be a role model." — Queen Latifah

Date: _____

_____

_____

_____

_____

_____

_____

_____

_____

_____

_____

_____

_____

_____

_____

_____

_____

_____

_____

_____

_____

_____

_____

_____

_____

_____

MY ACTION STATEMENT:

As a leader in my home, how can I encourage my children/family to be more active? What examples am I setting for them?

- **LaTasha Bester**

"As parents, we have the responsibility and the power to create a foundational love for nutritious foods that will influence our children's choices for decades to come, setting the stage for our children, grandchildren, and future generations to flourish in wellness and health." — Leah Borski

Date: _____

_____
_____
_____
_____
_____
_____
_____
_____
_____
_____
_____
_____
_____
_____
_____
_____
_____
_____
_____
_____
_____
_____
_____
_____
_____
_____

MY ACTION STATEMENT:

How can I INFLUENCE others to live a HEALTHY lifestyle?

- LaTasha Bester

"I don't know any other way to lead but by example."
- Don Shula

Date: _____

_____

_____

_____

_____

_____

_____

_____

_____

_____

_____

_____

_____

_____

_____

_____

_____

_____

_____

_____

_____

_____

_____

_____

_____

_____

_____

_____

_____

MY ACTION STATEMENT:

What are my thoughts about current issues (sex, gender, poverty, etc.)? Do they align with my faith principles?

-Laura Brown

"And be not conformed to this world: but be ye transformed by the renewing of your mind, that ye may prove what [is] that good, and acceptable, and perfect, will of God."

– Rom 12:2 KJV

Date: _____

_____

_____

_____

_____

_____

_____

_____

_____

_____

_____

_____

_____

_____

_____

_____

_____

_____

_____

_____

_____

_____

_____

_____

_____

_____

_____

_____

_____

_____

_____

_____

MY ACTION STATEMENT:

Is my life REFLECTIVE of what I share with others?

— Corri Bischer

"Live Your Message. Practice what you preach,. that's where credibility comes from." – John C Maxwell

Date: _____

_____
_____
_____
_____
_____
_____
_____
_____
_____
_____
_____
_____
_____
_____
_____
_____
_____
_____
_____
_____
_____
_____
_____

MY ACTION STATEMENT:

What are my economic priorities? Do they ALIGN with Kingdom priorities?

(does my bank statement reflect economic responsibility?)

- Laura Brown

"It's not your salary that makes you rich, it's your spending habits."
– Charles A. Jaffe

Date: _____

_____
_____
_____
_____
_____
_____
_____
_____
_____
_____
_____
_____
_____
_____
_____
_____
_____
_____
_____
_____
_____
_____
_____
_____
_____

MY ACTION STATEMENT:

HOW WELL DO I GIVE CONSTRUCTIVE CRITICISM TO THOSE WHO SEEK MY ADVICE?

-Laura Brown

"Criticism, like rain, should be gentle enough to nourish a man's growth without destroying his roots." – Frank A. Clark

Date: _____

_____
_____
_____
_____
_____
_____
_____
_____
_____
_____
_____
_____
_____
_____
_____
_____
_____
_____
_____
_____
_____
_____
_____
_____
_____
_____
_____
_____
_____
_____

MY ACTION STATEMENT:

Am I open to constructive criticism? Do I look for value in the words of others when they oppose or criticize me?

-Dr. David Banks & Laura Brown

"I like criticism. It makes you strong."
– LeBron James

Date: _____

_____
_____
_____
_____
_____
_____
_____
_____
_____
_____
_____
_____
_____
_____
_____
_____
_____
_____
_____
_____
_____
_____
_____
_____
_____
_____
_____
_____
_____
_____

MY ACTION STATEMENT:

INNER CRITIC #1

Describe your inner critic using your five senses

(sight, sound, smell, taste, touch).

- Laura Brown

"The critical voices in our own heads are far more vicious than what we might hear from the outside. Our "inside critics" have intimate knowledge of us and can zero in on our weakest spots."

— S.A.R.K. (a.k.a. Susan Ariel Rainbow Kennedy)

Date: _____

_____
_____
_____
_____
_____
_____
_____
_____
_____
_____
_____
_____
_____
_____
_____
_____
_____
_____
_____
_____
_____
_____
_____
_____
_____
_____
_____
_____

MY ACTION STATEMENT:

INNER CRITIC #2

What does your inner critic say to you? Create "snappy" comebacks to silence your inner critic.

-Laura Brown

"Remember, you have been criticizing yourself for years, and it hasn't worked. Try approving of yourself and see what happens."

— Louise L. Hay

Date: _____

_____

_____

_____

_____

_____

_____

_____

_____

_____

_____

_____

_____

_____

_____

_____

_____

_____

_____

_____

_____

_____

_____

_____

_____

_____

_____

_____

MY ACTION STATEMENT:

INNER CRITIC # 3
Tear this page out and send your inner critic away...

Option A: Put this page in an envelope and address it to fictional location. Do not put a return address! This is symbolic of blocking the inner critic from re-entry into your life.

Option B: Put this page in an envelope and address it to Inner Critic Island, P.O. Box 80092, Chattanooga, TN 37414. For the return address, you can use your initials or even a fictional name. Use your actual city and state. You may see your inner critic comebacks in our next book!

On the next page, describe how you feel after completing this mission

"Self-criticism and negative thoughts about yourself will attract people who reflect this back to you, showing critical behavior and can abuse you physically." — Hina Hashmi

Date: _____

_____

_____

_____

_____

_____

_____

_____

_____

_____

_____

_____

_____

_____

_____

_____

_____

_____

_____

_____

_____

_____

_____

_____

_____

_____

_____

MY ACTION STATEMENT:

INNER CHEERLEADER #1

Describe your inner cheerleader using your five senses
(sight, sound, smell, taste, touch).
- Laura Brown

"I will give thanks to You, for I am fearfully and wonderfully made; Wonderful are Your works, and my soul knows it very well."
— Psalm 139:14

"Cheering for ourselves with passion, and with a true sense of love and appreciation is not arrogant, it's actually required if we're going to live a life of fulfillment, gratitude, and meaning... Authentic self-appreciation is about loving, valuing, and honoring ourselves, our gifts and all of who we are — both light and dark." — Mike Robbins

Date: _____

_____
_____
_____
_____
_____
_____
_____
_____
_____
_____
_____
_____
_____
_____
_____
_____
_____
_____
_____
_____
_____
_____
_____
_____
_____
_____
_____
_____

MY ACTION STATEMENT:

INNER CHEERLEADER #2

What does your inner cheerleader say to you? Create at least five self-affirmation statements.

-Laura Brown

"As a man thinketh in his heart, so is he." – *Proverbs 23:7*

"One comes to believe whatever one repeats to oneself sufficiently often, whether the statement be true or false. It comes to be dominating thought in one's mind." – *Robert Collier*

Date: _____

_____

_____

_____

_____

_____

_____

_____

_____

_____

_____

_____

_____

_____

_____

_____

_____

_____

_____

_____

_____

_____

_____

_____

_____

_____

MY ACTION STATEMENT:

INNER CHEERLEADER # 3

Tear this page out and post it someplace you will see it daily. Optional Activity- Every cheerleader needs a team name and a mascot. Give YOUR team a name and describe/draw your team mascot.

"Affirmations are powerful and wonderful thoughts that serve you, your body, your immune system, your mind, and your spirit."

— Susan Barbara Apollon

Date: _____

MY TEAM MASCOT

MY ACTION STATEMENT:

HOW DO I RESPOND TO PERSONAL OR PROFESSIONAL FAILURES?

-Laura Brown & Janis Jackson

"The master has failed more times than the beginner has even tried." — Stephen McCranie

Date: _____

_____

_____

_____

_____

_____

_____

_____

_____

_____

_____

_____

_____

_____

_____

_____

_____

_____

_____

_____

_____

_____

_____

_____

_____

_____

_____

_____

MY ACTION STATEMENT:

Does my response to a failure in my life display tragedy or triumph?

- Frenise Mann

"Failure doesn't define you. It's what you do after you fail that determines whether you are a leader or a waste of perfectly good air." — Sabaa Tahir

Date: _____

_____
_____
_____
_____
_____
_____
_____
_____
_____
_____
_____
_____
_____
_____
_____
_____
_____
_____
_____
_____
_____
_____
_____
_____
_____
_____

MY ACTION STATEMENT:

DO I STAY FOCUSED WHEN EVERYTHING AROUND ME SEEMS TO BE FALLING APART? WHAT ARE THREE STRATEGIES I CAN USE TO STAY FOCUSED?

- Dammon Dunn

"When everything is moving and shifting, the only way to counteract chaos is stillness. When things feel extraordinary, strive for ordinary. When the surface is wavy, dive deeper for quieter waters." –Kristin Armstrong

"There is an immutable conflict at work in life and in business, a constant battle between peace and chaos. Neither can be mastered, but both can be influenced. How you go about that is the key to success." –Phil Knight

Date: _____

_____

_____

_____

_____

_____

_____

_____

_____

_____

_____

_____

_____

_____

_____

_____

_____

_____

_____

_____

_____

_____

_____

_____

_____

_____

_____

MY ACTION STATEMENT:

How difficult is it for me to admit when I am wrong?

- Dr. David Banks

"Mistakes are always forgivable if one has the courage to admit them."
– Bruce Lee

"A man must be big enough to admit his mistakes, smart enough to profit from them, and strong enough to correct them." – John C. Maxwell

Date: _____

_____

_____

_____

_____

_____

_____

_____

_____

_____

_____

_____

_____

_____

_____

_____

_____

_____

_____

_____

_____

_____

_____

_____

_____

MY ACTION STATEMENT:

What five WORDS come to MIND when I think about MONEY? Why?

-Laura Brown

"Money is not the only answer, but it makes a difference."
– Barack Obama

Date: _____

_____

_____

_____

_____

_____

_____

_____

_____

_____

_____

_____

_____

_____

_____

_____

_____

_____

_____

_____

_____

_____

_____

_____

_____

_____

_____

_____

MY ACTION STATEMENT:

Imagine your mind/heart is a storage room...

What mental/emotional clutter am I still HOLDING on to? Will it matter five years from now? Is it time to LET IT GO?

-Laura Brown

"I realize there's something incredibly honest about trees in winter, how they're experts at letting things go." — Jeffrey McDaniel

Date: _____

_____
_____
_____
_____
_____
_____
_____
_____
_____
_____
_____
_____
_____
_____
_____
_____
_____
_____
_____
_____
_____
_____
_____
_____
_____

MY ACTION STATEMENT:

How often do I stretch my faith or challenge myself beyond my present abilities?

-Laura Brown

"I can do all things through Christ which strengtheneth me."
-Philippians 4:13 (KJV)

"A man who believes that all things are possible approaches the unconventional with an open mind and a fearless heart." - Anonymous

Date: _____

_____
_____
_____
_____
_____
_____
_____
_____
_____
_____
_____
_____
_____
_____
_____
_____
_____
_____
_____
_____
_____
_____
_____
_____
_____
_____

MY ACTION STATEMENT:

How can I be more intentional about stimulating my creativity?

- Laura Brown

"To live a creative life, we must lose our fear of being wrong."

- Joseph Chilton Pearce

"Creativity is thinking up new things. Innovation is doing new things."

- Theodore Levitt

Date: _____

_____
_____
_____
_____
_____
_____
_____
_____
_____
_____
_____
_____
_____
_____
_____
_____
_____
_____
_____
_____
_____
_____
_____
_____
_____
_____

MY ACTION STATEMENT:

What NEW opportunities or connections am I cultivating or CREATING?

-Laura Brown

"Even when opportunity knocks, a man still has to get up off his seat and open the door." –Anonymous

Date: _____

_____

_____

_____

_____

_____

_____

_____

_____

_____

_____

_____

_____

_____

_____

_____

_____

_____

_____

_____

_____

_____

_____

_____

_____

_____

_____

_____

_____

MY ACTION STATEMENT:

What can I do now to maximize future opportunities?

— Patricia Robinson

"Opportunity is often missed because we are broadcasting when we should be tuning in." – Anonymous

Date: _____

_____

_____

_____

_____

_____

_____

_____

_____

_____

_____

_____

_____

_____

_____

_____

_____

_____

_____

_____

_____

_____

_____

_____

_____

_____

_____

_____

_____

_____

_____

_____

MY ACTION STATEMENT:

Who are my trusted advisors? To Whom do I go to vent and/or get encouragement?

-Dr. David Banks & Wayne Brown

"Learning to trust is one of life's most difficult tasks."
– Isaac Watts

"Iron sharpens iron, So one man sharpens another."
– Proverbs 27:17 (NASB)

Date: _____

_____
_____
_____
_____
_____
_____
_____
_____
_____
_____
_____
_____
_____
_____
_____
_____
_____
_____
_____
_____
_____
_____
_____
_____
_____
_____
_____

MY ACTION STATEMENT:

How can I create an inclusive environment to reproduce change agents?

– Dorothea Manley

"We need to give each other the space to grow, to be ourselves, to exercise our diversity. We need to give each other space so that we may both give and receive such beautiful things as ideas, openness, dignity, joy, healing, and inclusion." –Max de Pree

Date: _____

_____
_____
_____
_____
_____
_____
_____
_____
_____
_____
_____
_____
_____
_____
_____
_____
_____
_____
_____
_____
_____
_____
_____
_____
_____
_____

MY ACTION STATEMENT:

In what ways do I stretch my

GLOBAL MIND

M.A.P

(Mindset, Attitude, Perspective)

to understand/embrace those who

are different than me?

(culture, gender, beliefs, ethnicity, political, economics…)?

- Matthew Favors

"Culture makes people understand each other better. And if they understand each other better in their soul, it is easier to overcome the economic and political barriers. But first, they have to understand that their neighbour is, in the end, just like them, with the same problems, the same questions." –Paulo Coelho

Date: _____

_____
_____
_____
_____
_____
_____
_____
_____
_____
_____
_____
_____
_____
_____
_____
_____
_____
_____
_____
_____
_____
_____
_____
_____
_____
_____

MY ACTION STATEMENT:

THINK OF A LOCAL AND/OR GLOBAL ISSUE THAT BURDENS YOU. IF MONEY AND RESOURCES WERE NO ISSUE, HOW WOULD YOU SOLVE IT?

-Multiple Contributors

"There are no big problems, there are just a lot of little problems."

– Henry Ford

Date: _____

_____
_____
_____
_____
_____
_____
_____
_____
_____
_____
_____
_____
_____
_____
_____
_____
_____
_____
_____
_____
_____
_____
_____
_____
_____
_____

MY ACTION STATEMENT:

How often do I compare myself to others? How do I feel when I do this?

-Laura Brown

"If you stop comparing yourself with others and see your image in the mirror, you will realize how amazing you are." - Nishant Grover

"Compare yourself to others for inspiration, not competition."
— Bangambiki Habyarimana

Date: _____

_____
_____
_____
_____
_____
_____
_____
_____
_____
_____
_____
_____
_____
_____
_____
_____
_____
_____
_____
_____
_____
_____
_____
_____
_____
_____
_____
_____

MY ACTION STATEMENT:

Am I INTIMIDATED by other LEADERS in my field?
How can I be more INTENTIONAL about CULTIVATING relationships with other leaders?

-MULTIPLE CONTRIBUTORS

"Leaders are farmers; they cultivate human beings by adding values to them till they are fully grown as successful people for harvesting." — Israelmore Ayivor

Date: _____

_____

_____

_____

_____

_____

_____

_____

_____

_____

_____

_____

_____

_____

_____

_____

_____

_____

_____

_____

_____

_____

_____

_____

_____

_____

_____

_____

MY ACTION STATEMENT:

You will need a mirror for this reflection.

When I look in the mirror, who/what do I see?

-Laura Brown

"When you are trying to change the world. You don't have time to look in the mirror every day to feel as if something is wrong with you."
– Janelle Monae

Date: _____

_____

_____

_____

_____

_____

_____

_____

_____

_____

_____

_____

_____

_____

_____

_____

_____

_____

_____

_____

_____

_____

_____

_____

_____

_____

_____

_____

MY ACTION STATEMENT:

FOR WHAT PAST MISTAKES DO NEED TO FORGIVE MYSELF AND/OR OTHERS ?

-Laura Brown

"Forgiveness is the fragrance that the violet sheds on the heel that has crushed it." — Mark Twain

"The truth is unless you let go, unless you forgive yourself, unless you forgive the situation, unless you realize that the situation is over, you cannot move forward." — Steve Maraboli

Date: _____

_____
_____
_____
_____
_____
_____
_____
_____
_____
_____
_____
_____
_____
_____
_____
_____
_____
_____
_____
_____
_____
_____
_____
_____
_____
_____

MY ACTION STATEMENT:

WHAT ARE MY GREATEST STRENGTHS? WHY?

-Laura Brown

"Sometimes you don't realize your own strength until you come face to face with your greatest weakness."
— Susan Gale

Date: _____

_____

_____

_____

_____

_____

_____

_____

_____

_____

_____

_____

_____

_____

_____

_____

_____

_____

_____

_____

_____

_____

_____

_____

_____

_____

_____

MY ACTION STATEMENT:

What is my greatest fear? What is the source of this fear?

– DR. DAVID BANKS & VERNESSA DAVIS

"Your greatest fears are created by your imagination. Don't give in to them." –Winston Churchill

Date: _____

_____

_____

_____

_____

_____

_____

_____

_____

_____

_____

_____

_____

_____

_____

_____

_____

_____

_____

_____

_____

_____

_____

_____

_____

_____

_____

MY ACTION STATEMENT:

WHEN HAS FEAR HINDERED ME?

-Laura Brown

"Too many of us are not living our dreams because we are living our fears." – Les Brown

Date: _____

_____

_____

_____

_____

_____

_____

_____

_____

_____

_____

_____

_____

_____

_____

_____

_____

_____

_____

_____

_____

_____

_____

_____

_____

_____

_____

_____

_____

_____

MY ACTION STATEMENT:

When have I self-sabotaged opportunities due to fear of failure or fear of success?

- LJ Crawford & Alexis Willis

"Resistance, by definition, is self-sabotage." — Steven Pressfield

Date: _____

_____

_____

_____

_____

_____

_____

_____

_____

_____

_____

_____

_____

_____

_____

_____

_____

_____

_____

_____

_____

_____

_____

_____

_____

_____

_____

_____

_____

_____

MY ACTION STATEMENT:

Do I run away from PROBLEMS Or seek SOLUTIONS?

-Laura Brown

"Stop running away from your problems because that only increases the distance from the solution. Make it right today, tomorrow is too late."
– Anonymous

"Running away will never make you free." – Kenny Loggins

Date: _____

_____

_____

_____

_____

_____

_____

_____

_____

_____

_____

_____

_____

_____

_____

_____

_____

_____

_____

_____

_____

_____

_____

_____

_____

_____

MY ACTION STATEMENT:

What GIANTS am I facing right now? What is my plan to DEFEAT them?

-Laura Brown

"Don't be afraid to bite on a giant,
learn from the mosquito." — Bangambiki Habyarimana

Date: _____

_____
_____
_____
_____
_____
_____
_____
_____
_____
_____
_____
_____
_____
_____
_____
_____
_____
_____
_____
_____
_____
_____
_____
_____
_____
_____
_____
_____

MY ACTION STATEMENT:

What steps can I take to cultivate BOLDNESS in my relationships/friendships?

– Corri Bischer

"Be bold, be brave enough to be your true self."

– Queen Latifah

Date: _____

_____

_____

_____

_____

_____

_____

_____

_____

_____

_____

_____

_____

_____

_____

_____

_____

_____

_____

_____

_____

_____

_____

_____

_____

_____

_____

_____

_____

_____

MY ACTION STATEMENT:

Who are the five people/groups I spend the most time with? How do they motivate me? How do I motivate them?

-Laura Brown

"It's hard to stay motivated when the people around you are not. Choose your friends wisely." – Anonymous

Date: _____

_____
_____
_____
_____
_____
_____
_____
_____
_____
_____
_____
_____
_____
_____
_____
_____
_____
_____
_____
_____
_____
_____
_____
_____
_____
_____
_____
_____

MY ACTION STATEMENT:

As a leader, how can I cultivate accountability in myself and those I lead?

-Laura Brown

"Each day you are leading by example.
Whether you realize it or not or whether it's positive or
negative, you are influencing those around you." —Rob Liano

Date: _____

_____

_____

_____

_____

_____

_____

_____

_____

_____

_____

_____

_____

_____

_____

_____

_____

_____

_____

_____

_____

_____

_____

_____

_____

_____

_____

_____

_____

_____

MY ACTION STATEMENT:

WHAT ARE SOME VICTORIES I HAVE HAD IN LIFE?

-Laura Brown

"I may not have avoided certain wounds in my life, but I do appreciate these scars because they are a constant reminder of my victories."
– Gugu Mona

Date: _____

_____
_____
_____
_____
_____
_____
_____
_____
_____
_____
_____
_____
_____
_____
_____
_____
_____
_____
_____
_____
_____
_____
_____
_____
_____
_____
_____
_____

MY ACTION STATEMENT:

How do I CELEBRATE the success of others? Do I CELEBRATE my own success just as much? If not, why?

-Laura Brown

"Celebrate each accomplishment on your way to reaching your goal. Each challenge conquered whether large or small is a positive step to greatness."
– Robert Cheeke

Date: _____

_____
_____
_____
_____
_____
_____
_____
_____
_____
_____
_____
_____
_____
_____
_____
_____
_____
_____
_____
_____
_____
_____
_____
_____
_____
_____
_____
_____

MY ACTION STATEMENT:

Who gets the credit for my personal or professional success?

- Gary Bloodsaw

True humility and fear of the LORD lead to riches, honor, and long life.
– Proverbs 22:4 (NLT)

"Don't let success go to your head. Remember,
when success comes, walk in humility." – Bill Newman

Date: _____

_____
_____
_____
_____
_____
_____
_____
_____
_____
_____
_____
_____
_____
_____
_____
_____
_____
_____
_____
_____
_____
_____
_____
_____
_____
_____

MY ACTION STATEMENT:

HOW DO I RESPOND WHEN MY ENEMIES OR MY COMPETITORS SUCCEED?

-Laura Brown

"Hatred of someone else's accomplishment is a glaring sign of insecurity. Respect success and do your best to achieve even more than your rival."
- Anurag Prakash Ray

Date: _____

_____

_____

_____

_____

_____

_____

_____

_____

_____

_____

_____

_____

_____

_____

_____

_____

_____

_____

_____

_____

_____

_____

_____

_____

_____

_____

_____

_____

MY ACTION STATEMENT:

What unproductive habits do I want to break?

-Laura Brown

"A change in bad habits leads to a change in life." – Jenny Craig

Date: _____

_____

_____

_____

_____

_____

_____

_____

_____

_____

_____

_____

_____

_____

_____

_____

_____

_____

_____

_____

_____

_____

_____

_____

_____

_____

_____

_____

MY ACTION STATEMENT:

What productive habits do I want to cultivate?

-Laura Brown

"Good habits, once established are just as hard
to break as are bad habits." – Robert Puller

Date: _____

_____
_____
_____
_____
_____
_____
_____
_____
_____
_____
_____
_____
_____
_____
_____
_____
_____
_____
_____
_____
_____
_____
_____
_____
_____
_____
_____
_____
_____
_____

MY ACTION STATEMENT:

HOW DO I
RESPOND
TO PERSONAL AND/OR PROFESSIONAL
CRISIS?

-April Boozer

"If you don't have a spiritual practice in place when times are good, you can't expect to suddenly develop one during a moment of crisis."
– Doug Coupland

Date: _____

_____
_____
_____
_____
_____
_____
_____
_____
_____
_____
_____
_____
_____
_____
_____
_____
_____
_____
_____
_____
_____
_____
_____
_____
_____
_____
_____

MY ACTION STATEMENT:

Am I willing to SEE the TRUTH?

— Erika Hughes

"And ye shall know the truth, and the truth shall make you free."
John 8:32 (KJV)

Date: _____

_____
_____
_____
_____
_____
_____
_____
_____
_____
_____
_____
_____
_____
_____
_____
_____
_____
_____
_____
_____
_____
_____
_____
_____
_____
_____
_____

MY ACTION STATEMENT:

What can I do today to be spiritually courageous?

-Corri Bischer

"His voice leads us not into timid discipleship but into bold witness."
- Charles Stanley

Date: _____

_____

_____

_____

_____

_____

_____

_____

_____

_____

_____

_____

_____

_____

_____

_____

_____

_____

_____

_____

_____

_____

_____

_____

_____

_____

_____

_____

_____

MY ACTION STATEMENT:

What can I do to help my community recover?

– Reginald White

"In every community, there is work to be done. In every nation, there are wounds to heal. In every heart, there is the power to do it."

– Marianne Williamson

Date: _____

_____

_____

_____

_____

_____

_____

_____

_____

_____

_____

_____

_____

_____

_____

_____

_____

_____

_____

_____

_____

_____

_____

_____

_____

_____

_____

MY ACTION STATEMENT:

WHAT ARE THE FIVE TOP QUALITIES OF EFFECTIVE LEADERSHIP? HOW CAN I CULTIVATE THEM IN MYSELF AND OTHERS?

- Maiya Banks, April Boozer, & Reginald Favors Sr.

"Leadership is unlocking people's potential to become better." – Bill Bradley

Date: _____

_____

_____

_____

_____

_____

_____

_____

_____

_____

_____

_____

_____

_____

_____

_____

_____

_____

_____

_____

_____

_____

_____

_____

_____

_____

_____

MY ACTION STATEMENT:

Have I done all I can to IMPACT my family members?

-Carlos Mann

"Family means no one gets left behind or forgotten."
– David Ogden Stiers

Date: _____

_____

_____

_____

_____

_____

_____

_____

_____

_____

_____

_____

_____

_____

_____

_____

_____

_____

_____

_____

_____

_____

_____

_____

_____

_____

_____

MY ACTION STATEMENT:

On a scale of 1-10, how do I rate my physical health?

Poor	Fair	Good	Very Good	Excellent
1 2	3 4	5 6	7 8	9 10

Couch Potato   **Regular Exercise**

Does it align with biblical standards?

What areas need improvement?

-LaTasha Bester

"Beloved, I pray that in all respects you may prosper and be in good health, just as your soul prospers." – III John 1:2

"Take care of your body. It's the only place you have to live." – Jim Rohn

Date: _____

_____

_____

_____

_____

_____

_____

_____

_____

_____

_____

_____

_____

_____

_____

_____

_____

_____

_____

_____

_____

_____

_____

_____

_____

_____

_____

_____

_____

_____

MY ACTION STATEMENT:

WHAT ARE MY TOP THREE FITNESS GOALS? HOW CAN I REACH THEM?

- LaTasha Bester

"To keep the body in good health is a duty; otherwise we shall not be able to keep our mind strong and clear." – Buddha

Date: _____

_____

_____

_____

_____

_____

_____

_____

_____

_____

_____

_____

_____

_____

_____

_____

_____

_____

_____

_____

_____

_____

_____

_____

_____

_____

MY ACTION STATEMENT:

HOW DO I DETERMINE THE DIFFERENCE BETWEEN WHAT IS URGENT AND WHAT IS IMPORTANT?

-Dr. David Banks

"What is important is seldom urgent, and what is urgent is seldom important." – Dwight D. Eisenhower

Date: _____

_____
_____
_____
_____
_____
_____
_____
_____
_____
_____
_____
_____
_____
_____
_____
_____
_____
_____
_____
_____
_____
_____
_____
_____
_____
_____
_____
_____

MY ACTION STATEMENT:

WHAT PERSONAL, MINISTRY, AND PROFESSIONAL BOUNDARIES? HAVE I ESTABLISHED?

-Laura Brown

"Boundary setting is really a huge part of time management."
– Jim Loehr

"Lack of boundaries invites lack of respect." — Anonymous

Date: _____

_____

_____

_____

_____

_____

_____

_____

_____

_____

_____

_____

_____

_____

_____

_____

_____

_____

_____

_____

_____

_____

_____

_____

_____

_____

_____

_____

_____

_____

MY ACTION STATEMENT:

Am I intentional about scheduling "Me Time"? Why or Why not?

- Angela Daniels

"Prioritize self-care & incorporate a minimum of 60 mins 'ME TIME' into your daily routine. Yes, there are enough hours in the day. NO EXCUSES." — Miya Yamanouchi

Date: _____

_____
_____
_____
_____
_____
_____
_____
_____
_____
_____
_____
_____
_____
_____
_____
_____
_____
_____
_____
_____
_____
_____
_____
_____
_____
_____
_____

MY ACTION STATEMENT:

HOW DO I FEEL ABOUT THE WAY I MANAGE MY TIME?

– CHAFEE DUNN

"How you spend your time is more important than how you spend your money. Money mistakes can be corrected, but time is gone forever."
–David Norris

Date: _____

_____

_____

_____

_____

_____

_____

_____

_____

_____

_____

_____

_____

_____

_____

_____

_____

_____

_____

_____

_____

_____

_____

_____

_____

_____

_____

_____

_____

_____

MY ACTION STATEMENT:

Am I ENTHUSIASTIC about my WORK?

Why or Why not?

- JOHN DICKERT

"Inspirational leaders need to have a winning mentality in order to inspire respect. It is hard to trust in the leadership of someone who is half-hearted about their purpose, or only sporadic in focus or enthusiasm."

– Sebastian Coe

Date: _____

_____

_____

_____

_____

_____

_____

_____

_____

_____

_____

_____

_____

_____

_____

_____

_____

_____

_____

_____

_____

_____

_____

_____

_____

_____

_____

_____

MY ACTION STATEMENT:

HOW WELL DO I MANAGE ENERGY-DRAINING EMOTIONS (GRIEF, ANGER, BITTERNESS...?)

- Trina McKinney

"Treat negative emotions like negative people. Acknowledge their presence and make whatever changes are required to remove them from your life."
–Anonymous

Date: _____

_____

_____

_____

_____

_____

_____

_____

_____

_____

_____

_____

_____

_____

_____

_____

_____

_____

_____

_____

_____

_____

_____

_____

_____

_____

_____

MY ACTION STATEMENT:

Am I leading out of PASSION or FRUSTRATION?

- Dr. David Banks & Angela Daniels

"Our fatigue is often caused not by work, but by worry, frustration, and resentment." – Dale Carnegie

Date: _____

_____

_____

_____

_____

_____

_____

_____

_____

_____

_____

_____

_____

_____

_____

_____

_____

_____

_____

_____

_____

_____

_____

_____

_____

_____

_____

_____

_____

_____

_____

MY ACTION STATEMENT:

WHAT OR WHO ARE MY GREATEST "TIME THIEVES"?

-Laura Brown

"Remember that lost time does not return."
– Thomas A. Kempis

Date: _____

_____

_____

_____

_____

_____

_____

_____

_____

_____

_____

_____

_____

_____

_____

_____

_____

_____

_____

_____

_____

_____

_____

_____

_____

_____

_____

_____

_____

_____

MY ACTION STATEMENT:

If I were a book what would people read? What would be the title?

~ Sylvia Banks

''Your life is a book; make it a bestseller.'' – Shanon Grey

Date: _____

_____

_____

_____

_____

_____

_____

_____

_____

_____

_____

_____

_____

_____

_____

_____

_____

_____

_____

_____

_____

_____

_____

_____

_____

_____

_____

MY ACTION STATEMENT:

How have I used my influence to impact others?

-Dr. Sharon Cannon & Reginald Favors Sr.

"Certain individuals and events impact on our lives and leave their mark on us. Some a feeling of happiness and contentment, while others hit us like bullets to the heart." – Rashida Rowe

Date: _____

_____
_____
_____
_____
_____
_____
_____
_____
_____
_____
_____
_____
_____
_____
_____
_____
_____
_____
_____
_____
_____
_____
_____
_____
_____
_____

MY ACTION STATEMENT:

WHAT HINDERS ME FROM MOVING FORWARD?

– MARY "PRECIOUS" SMITH

"You need to have faith in yourself. Be brave and take risks. You don't have to have it all figured out to move forward." - Roy T. Bennett

Date: _____

_____

_____

_____

_____

_____

_____

_____

_____

_____

_____

_____

_____

_____

_____

_____

_____

_____

_____

_____

_____

_____

_____

_____

_____

_____

_____

_____

_____

MY ACTION STATEMENT:

WHEN HAVE I FELT MOST POWERFUL?

-Laura Brown

''I always thought I was powerful since I was a kid.''

– Zaha Hadid

Date: _____

_____

_____

_____

_____

_____

_____

_____

_____

_____

_____

_____

_____

_____

_____

_____

_____

_____

_____

_____

_____

_____

_____

_____

_____

_____

_____

_____

MY ACTION STATEMENT:

What are my expectations of myself as a leader?

Are they realistic?

Do they challenge me?

- April Boozer

"Don't lower your expectations to meet your performance. Raise your level of performance to meet your expectations." – Ralph Marston

Date: _____

_____

_____

_____

_____

_____

_____

_____

_____

_____

_____

_____

_____

_____

_____

_____

_____

_____

_____

_____

_____

_____

_____

_____

_____

_____

_____

MY ACTION STATEMENT:

How do I handle people's failure to meet my expectations?
How can I better set and communicate realistic expectations?
-Laura Brown & April Boozer

"I think sometimes you have high expectations for people because you have high expectations for yourself." – Gisele Bundchen

Date: _____

_____

_____

_____

_____

_____

_____

_____

_____

_____

_____

_____

_____

_____

_____

_____

_____

_____

_____

_____

_____

_____

_____

_____

_____

_____

_____

_____

_____

MY ACTION STATEMENT:

Why do I doubt myself?

– Dr. David Banks

''Doubt kills more dreams than failure ever will.'' – Suzy Kassem

Date: _____

_____
_____
_____
_____
_____
_____
_____
_____
_____
_____
_____
_____
_____
_____
_____
_____
_____
_____
_____
_____
_____
_____
_____
_____
_____
_____

MY ACTION STATEMENT:

Do I live with integrity?

Based upon my past track record would I:

hire me, rent to me, loan me money, trust me with responsibilities, go into business with me? Why?

-Dr. David Banks & Laura Brown

"Character is much easier kept than recovered." — Thomas Paine

Date: _____

_____
_____
_____
_____
_____
_____
_____
_____
_____
_____
_____
_____
_____
_____
_____
_____
_____
_____
_____
_____
_____
_____
_____
_____
_____
_____
_____

MY ACTION STATEMENT:

How would I rate my personal and business reputation?

Poor	Fair	Good	Very Good	Excellent
1 2	3 4	5 6	7 8	9 10

Needs Improvement   **Above Reproach**

What areas need improvement?
-Laura Brown

"A reputation once broken may possibly be repaired, but the world will always keep their eyes on the spot where the crack was." — Joseph Hall

Date: _____

_____
_____
_____
_____
_____
_____
_____
_____
_____
_____
_____
_____
_____
_____
_____
_____
_____
_____
_____
_____
_____
_____
_____
_____
_____
_____
_____
_____
_____

MY ACTION STATEMENT:

What thought and behavior PATTERNS am I willing to change?

— ERIKA HUGHES

"We change our behavior when the pain of staying the same becomes greater than the pain of changing."
-Dr. Henry Cloud & Dr. John Townsend

Date: _____

_____

_____

_____

_____

_____

_____

_____

_____

_____

_____

_____

_____

_____

_____

_____

_____

_____

_____

_____

_____

_____

_____

_____

_____

_____

_____

_____

MY ACTION STATEMENT:

What STEPS can I take to get my RESOURCES to line up with my VISION?

– Geoffrey Moore

"Chase the vision, not the money, the money will end up following you."
– Tony Hsieh

Date: _____

_____

_____

_____

_____

_____

_____

_____

_____

_____

_____

_____

_____

_____

_____

_____

_____

_____

_____

_____

_____

_____

_____

_____

_____

_____

_____

_____

MY ACTION STATEMENT:

How can I

LIVE

"Outside of the

BOX"?

–Dr. David Banks

"It isn't enough to think outside the box. Thinking is passive. Get used to acting outside the box." - Tim Ferriss

Date: _____

_____

_____

_____

_____

_____

_____

_____

_____

_____

_____

_____

_____

_____

_____

_____

_____

_____

_____

_____

_____

_____

_____

_____

_____

_____

_____

_____

_____

_____

_____

MY ACTION STATEMENT:

What valuable investments have I made in myself

~ Sylvia Banks & Stephanie Dickert

"It hurts...when the world won't invest in you. But it's excruciating, almost more than you can bear when you don't believe and invest in yourself."
– Julia Cameron

Date: _____

_____

_____

_____

_____

_____

_____

_____

_____

_____

_____

_____

_____

_____

_____

_____

_____

_____

_____

_____

_____

_____

_____

_____

_____

_____

MY ACTION STATEMENT:

HOW CAN I NURTURE CREATIVE THINKING IN MYSELF AND OTHERS TO EXPAND OUR VISION?

- **Stephanie Dickert**

"If you want to build a ship, don't herd people together to collect wood and don't assign them tasks and work, but rather teach them to long for the endless immensity of the sea." – Antoine de Saint-Exupery

Date: _____

_____

_____

_____

_____

_____

_____

_____

_____

_____

_____

_____

_____

_____

_____

_____

_____

_____

_____

_____

_____

_____

_____

_____

_____

_____

_____

MY ACTION STATEMENT:

When was the last time I PUSHED myself to do something that seems IMPOSSIBLE?

- Dr. David Banks & Patricia Robinson

"The only way to discover the limits of the possible is to go beyond them into the impossible." - Arthur C. Clarke

"For nothing will be impossible with God." - Luke 1:37 NASB

Date: _____

_____

_____

_____

_____

_____

_____

_____

_____

_____

_____

_____

_____

_____

_____

_____

_____

_____

_____

_____

_____

_____

_____

_____

_____

_____

_____

_____

_____

MY ACTION STATEMENT:

What idea(s) have I delayed implementing because of "analysis paralysis" or "worst-case scenario" fears?

-Laura Brown

"Thinking will not overcome fear but action will." — Clement Stone

Date: _____

_____
_____
_____
_____
_____
_____
_____
_____
_____
_____
_____
_____
_____
_____
_____
_____
_____
_____
_____
_____
_____
_____
_____
_____
_____
_____

MY ACTION STATEMENT:

How can I CHALLENGE myself to get to the next LEVEL?

– Sada' Torrey

"In order to take our lives to the next level, we must realize that the same pattern of thinking that has gotten us to where we are now will not get us to where we want to go." – Tony Robbins

Date: _____

_____

_____

_____

_____

_____

_____

_____

_____

_____

_____

_____

_____

_____

_____

_____

_____

_____

_____

_____

_____

_____

_____

_____

_____

_____

_____

_____

_____

_____

_____

MY ACTION STATEMENT:

WHAT WAS THE LAST BOOK I READ? WHAT VALUABLE LESSON DID I LEARN FROM IT?

- Dr. David Banks

"A capacity, and taste, for reading gives access to whatever has already been discovered by others." – Abraham Lincoln

Date: _____

_____
_____
_____
_____
_____
_____
_____
_____
_____
_____
_____
_____
_____
_____
_____
_____
_____
_____
_____
_____
_____
_____
_____
_____
_____
_____
_____
_____

MY ACTION STATEMENT:

DO I LOOK FOR WAYS TO SUCCEED EVEN IF THE WAY AHEAD IS NOT CLEAR?

- John Dickert

"Travelers, there is no path, paths are made by walking."
- Antonio Machado

Date: _____

_____
_____
_____
_____
_____
_____
_____
_____
_____
_____
_____
_____
_____
_____
_____
_____
_____
_____
_____
_____
_____
_____
_____
_____
_____
_____
_____

MY ACTION STATEMENT:

In what ways do I invest in others?

~ Sylvia Banks & Stephanie Dickert

"The true meaning of life is to plant trees, under whose shade you do not expect to sit." – Nelson Henderson

Date: _____

_____

_____

_____

_____

_____

_____

_____

_____

_____

_____

_____

_____

_____

_____

_____

_____

_____

_____

_____

_____

_____

_____

_____

_____

_____

_____

_____

MY ACTION STATEMENT:

AM I SEEKING AND DEVELOPING SUCCESSORS? WHO? HOW?

- Dr. David Banks

"True leaders don't invest in buildings. Jesus never built a building. They invest in people...Because success without a successor is failure. So, your legacy should not be in buildings, programs, or projects; your legacy must be in people." – Myles Munroe

Date: _____

_____

_____

_____

_____

_____

_____

_____

_____

_____

_____

_____

_____

_____

_____

_____

_____

_____

_____

_____

_____

_____

_____

_____

_____

_____

_____

_____

MY ACTION STATEMENT:

As a Leader, Am I

CONTROLLING

my followers or

CREATING

future leaders.

-Dr. David Banks

"The function of leadership is to produce more leaders, not more followers."
– Ralph Nader

Date: _____

_____

_____

_____

_____

_____

_____

_____

_____

_____

_____

_____

_____

_____

_____

_____

_____

_____

_____

_____

_____

_____

_____

_____

_____

_____

MY ACTION STATEMENT:

In what ways do I allow God's possessions to be a blessing to others?

– Anonymous

"One who is gracious to a poor man lends to the LORD, and He will repay him for his good deed." – Proverbs 19:17 (NASB)

Date: _____

_____

_____

_____

_____

_____

_____

_____

_____

_____

_____

_____

_____

_____

_____

_____

_____

_____

_____

_____

_____

_____

_____

_____

_____

_____

_____

_____

MY ACTION STATEMENT:

Am I afraid to

LIVE

on top?

– Dr. David Banks

"Fear comes in two packages fear of failure, and sometimes, fear of success." – Tom Kite

Date: _____

_____

_____

_____

_____

_____

_____

_____

_____

_____

_____

_____

_____

_____

_____

_____

_____

_____

_____

_____

_____

_____

_____

_____

_____

_____

_____

MY ACTION STATEMENT:

What legacy do I want to leave for future generations?

-Laura Brown

"The graveyard is the richest place on earth, because it is here that you will find all the hopes and dreams that were never fulfilled, the books that were never written, the songs that were never sung, the inventions that were never shared, the cures that were never discovered, all because someone was too afraid to take that first step..." -Les Brown

Date: _____

_____

_____

_____

_____

_____

_____

_____

_____

_____

_____

_____

_____

_____

_____

_____

_____

_____

_____

_____

_____

_____

_____

_____

_____

_____

_____

MY ACTION STATEMENT:

WHAT AM I DOING NOW TO ENSURE I LEAVE A POSITIVE indelible mark ON THE WORLD FOR FUTURE GENERATIONS?

-Frenise Mann

Challenge: Design your own "indelible mark" on the next page!

"It is very sad to me that some people are so intent on leaving their mark on the world, that they don't care if that mark is a scar." — John Green

Date: _____

_____
_____
_____
_____
_____
_____
_____
_____
_____
_____
_____
_____
_____

Use this space to design your own "indelible mark".

MY ACTION STATEMENT:

How is my thinking DIFFERENT after completing this Journal?

-Laura Brown

"Change is the end result of all true learning."
– Leo Buscaglia

Date: _____

_____
_____
_____
_____
_____
_____
_____
_____
_____
_____
_____
_____
_____
_____
_____
_____
_____
_____
_____
_____
_____
_____
_____
_____
_____
_____

MY ACTION STATEMENT:

Use this space to write your own questions. We would love for you to share your questions with us. Go to www.empowermentembassy.com and send us your questions.
You may just see your question in an updated version of the book!

_____

_____

_____

_____

_____

_____

_____

_____

_____

_____

_____

_____

_____

Index

(Contributors and Quote References)

C

D

E

M

N

O

P

Q

R

S

T

ABOUT THE CONTRIBUTORS

DAVID BANKS, PH. D. is a Certified Behavioral Consultant, a Professional Speaker, and Certified Professional Coach. Dr. Banks has a passion for empowering people to move from survival to success. He has expertise in Relationships, Leadership Development, Motivation and Purpose Discovery. Dr. Banks has authored a marriage book; "Draw Me Close." He lives in Chattanooga, TN with his lovely bride, Sylvia Banks, and their three children. Contact Dr. Banks at drdb@noblesuccessll.com or visit www.facebook.com/NoblesuccessLLC.

MAIYA DESTA BANKS is a sophomore at Banks Academy of Excellence. She is the Business owner of Desta Creations and an accomplished ballet dancer. Maiya lives in Chattanooga, TN with her parents Dr. David & Sylvia Banks and her two brothers, Benjamin and Caleb.

SYLVIA BANKS is a teacher, mentor, and author. She is passionate about helping women excel in every area of their lives. Sylvia has developed and taught two courses: Women of Excellence and Time for ORDER. She is an author of a book; "7 Pillars of a Noble Woman". She is originally from India and was born and raised in Ethiopia. Sylvia lives in Chattanooga, TNe with her husband and three children.

LATASHA BESTER is a Toledo, OH native who currently resides in Chattanooga, TN. She is the founder of Fitness is Freedom a personal and family fitness training business. She has two beautiful daughters who enjoy competing in Spartan Races with her. You can contact LaTasha at fitnessisfreedom84@yahoo.com, on Instagram @freedomfitness84, and on Facebook @ Fitness is Freedom or LaTasha Bester

TORRI BISCHER is an author, speaker, strategist, and trainer for The Wakesh Foundation. She helps others discover strategies to ignite and inspire the creativity in our youth. It is her goal to help them become purpose-driven adults with problem-solving skills for world issues. She is the author of "Igniting and Inspiring Life-long Learners." Corri is originally from Pasadena, CA and now lives in Chattanooga, TN. For more information about Corri go to www.wakeshfoundation.org or email her at wakeshfoundation@yahoo.com.

GARY BLOODSAW JR. was born in Monroe, GA to Gary Bloodsaw Sr. and Christine Bloodsaw. Gary has been married to Rosalyn Bloodsaw (Simpson) for over 30 years, and they reside in Chattanooga, TN. Gary and Rosalyn have two children and one grandson. Gary is a graduate of the University of Tennessee at Chattanooga, where he received his bachelor's degree in Education. He went on to earn his Master's degree in Curriculum from the University of Phoenix. Gary has been working as a public-school teacher for over 30 years

APRIL ELLIS BOOZER was born and raised in Shelby, NC. She is the Executive director of a non-profit organization Father to the Fatherless (F2F), which provides services and resources to at risk youth and adults. April currently resides in Chattanooga, TN. You can contact April at www.f2fchattanooga.org, aboozer@f2fchattanooga.org or on Facebook @Father to the Fatherless

LAURA BROWN, affectionally known as "Coach Laura", is an author, teacher, speaker, creative strategist, and creator of The Serious Writers' Accountability Training (S.W.A.T.) Camp where she helps aspiring authors create literary legacies and unleash their inner super hero through writing. She is the author of The Psalm 119 DevArtJournal and Color Me Delighted Psalm 119 Coloring Book Prayer Journal. Laura is a native of Toledo, OH and now resides in Chattanooga, TN with her husband, Wayne. They enjoy planning surprise PopPop and Nanna adventures for their two granddaughters. You can contact Laura at coachlaurabrown@swatbookcamp.com or www.coachlaurabrown.com.

WAYNE S. BROWN is an author, mentor, professional speaker, and community leader in Chattanooga. He was born in Albany, GA and is a 30-year US Air Force veteran. Wayne has a Bachelor of Science and a Bachelor of Biblical Studies degree. He is the author of "Listen – Wisdom and Wit for the Next Generation." You can contact Wayne for speaking engagements at wayne@BridgeNTheGap.com or go to www.BridgeNTheGap.com

DR. SHARON A. CANNON is a soldier for the Lord. She has received many accolades relative to spreading the word through her teaching while being an instructor, motivator, mentor, business woman, speaker. She is the author of "Black People of the Bible" and "Women of the Bible: The Good, the Bad & Ugly...Then and Now" available in paperback and audiobook. Contact Dr. Cannon at www.sacpr.com or sacpr@bellsouth.net.

LJ CRAWFORD is an author, keynote speaker, corporate sales professional, and founder of LJC Motivations. She was born and raised in Chattanooga, TN. She received her B.S in Business Management. LJ is an expert Personal Power Developer. She helps individuals understand they were designed for a purpose in every position they hold. LJ is the author of "The Master Relationship Builder-Relationship Building Through the Eyes of the Employee", "Silent Screams" and has also co-authored "Business Leader Success" which reached Kindle #1. Contact LJ at www.ljcmotivations.net or www.linkedin.com/in/lisajcrawford

STEPHANIE DICKERT is an author, accountant, and certified Quick Books Pro Advisor. A reformed banker-turned-accountant, Stephanie is an entrepreneur and owner of "Stewardship for Life" accounting firm. She developed the "Money 101" program and is the author of "We the Consumers: What Happened to We the People?" Stephanie is a Chattanooga, Tennessee native and now lives in Georgia with her husband, John, and their daughter Faith. They operate a 40-acre working farm raising produce and cattle.

VANESSA DAVIS-PORRAS was born and raised in New York and studied at Suffolk Community College and Briarcliffe Secretarial School along with concentrating on Cosmetology at Brookhaven (BOCES). She is a pioneer for entrepreneurship, and she uses her purpose to encourage, uplift and motivate people in the word of God. Vernessa now lives in Chattanooga, TN.

DAMMON D. DUNN SR is an entrepreneur, mentor, leader, father, who thru his business (TopNotch) seeks to help men transform their lives just as he specializes in automobile transformation by striving to lead by example. Dammon is from Bowling Green, KY and now resides in Chattanooga, TN. For more information, contact Dammon at topnotchmobiledetail@mail.com or www.ddunn08@mail.com.

GABRIELLE THAFEE DUNN is a graduate of the University of Tennessee at Chattanooga. She is a founding board member of Stepping Stones Ministry, a ministry dedicated to housing homeless families, and the JT Memorial Scholarship. She volunteers her time with the Kingdom Worshippers Praise Dance Team. You can contact Gabrielle on LinkedIn and FB.

REGINALD FAVORS SR. is a mentor for the non-profit group Father to the Fatherless. Reginald also owns a Primerica Financial Services business. He and his wife, Donna, reside in Chattanooga, TN and they have two sons, Reggie Jr. and Matthew Favors.

CARLOS MANN is a native of Wisconsin and currently lives in Chattanooga, TN. He is happily married to his bride, Frenise Mann. He has two daughters, Kayla and Victoria and a beautiful granddaughter. He is a graduate of ILD Leadership School and certified as a City Strategist. Carlos is the owner and CEO of Mann Power, a mobile detailing, carpet, and upholstery cleaning service. Carlos and his wife, Frenise, are certified as marriage coaches through Prepare/Enrich. He is also a minister. His purpose and passion in life is to encourage, motivate and empower people who have been mistreated and overlooked because of race, social or economic status.

FRENISE MANN is a women's mentor, speaker, life coach, author, and multifaceted executive. She is the founder and owner of Mann Financial Coaching and Indelible Legacy. Frenise lives in Chattanooga, TN. She believes life should be lived without regrets, intentionally, and on purpose. Contact Frenise @ frenisemann@gmail.com.

DOROTHEA R. MANLEY is a native of Paducah, KY. She was granted her ministerial license in 1997 and earned a Bachelor's degree in Administrative Studies from Roosevelt University in Chicago, IL in 2011. Dorothea is an aspiring life-coach, purpose discovery specialist, and strategic interventionist, whose passion is helping people move beyond barriers to their personal and professional success. She has served as a missionary and volunteer in Africa, Chicago, and Chattanooga.

TRINA MCKINNEY was born and raised in Chicago, IL and now lives in Chattanooga, TN. She is a professional make-up artist and has worked in the customer service industry for over 20 years.

PATRICIA ROBINSON lives in Chattanooga, TN, where she is a fruitful real estate investor and mommy to her daughter, Milla. She has finally asked and answered the questions in her head...do I have what it takes? Her answer- In spades! Dormant no more, see her crazy, creative, and courageous sides revealed in her first children's book coming March 2018. You can contact her at inspadesnow@gmail.com.

MARY "PRECIOUS" SMITH is a dedicated mother, grandmother, and self-taught seamstress. She lives in Chattanooga, TN. Contact Mary at smitprecious@gmail.com.

SADA' TORREY is a wife, mother, entrepreneur, and author. She is the creator of SUPERGirls Summer Camp, a leadership camp for girls 6-17 years old, and Womanhood Conquered, where she helps women find the tools and strategies needed to move forward and create order in their lives. She is the author of Pillow Talk, a 365-day journal for couples to promote deeper intimacy through communication and journaling together. Sada' was born in Atlanta, Georgia and currently resides in Chattanooga, TN.

KATHY T. WHITE lives in Chattanooga, TN. She has a Master's Degree in Vocational Rehabilitation. Kathy provides employment assistance for persons with disabilities, and pre-employment transitional services for youth.

REGINALD 1. WHITE resides in Chattanooga, TN. He has an A.S. degree in Social Work. Reginald has a passion for providing assistance to the elderly and persons with disabilities.

TARRELL T. WHITESIDE is a native of Chattanooga, TN. He attended Auburn University and The University of Tennessee at Chattanooga where he received a B.S. in Industrial Engineering. Tarrell is a coach, mentor, and minister. Tarrell is also a sports official, and he strives to encourage youth to live to their full potential.

ALEXIS (AJ) WILLIS is an IRONMAN competitor, writer, and entrepreneur. She is the founder of Natural Beautiful Me, a platform to empower women to embrace their natural beauty and value their identity. Alexis is a connector in the community and has been dubbed as The Startup Maven. Currently, she is Director of Strategic Initiatives and Business Support for both The Company Lab and LAUNCH and has helped jump start dozens of ideas and businesses. Her most challenging and rewarding work is raising her daughter, Riley aka "Boom", as a single mother.

www.ingramcontent.com/pod-product-compliance
Lightning Source LLC
Chambersburg PA
CBHW060738050426
42449CB00008B/1262